Yoga for Cats

by **Talia Katasanda**
(*nom-de-chat of Erica Rutherford*)

1988
Ragweed Press
Charlottetown

Copyright, ©, 1984, 1988, Erica Rutherford

ISBN 0-920304-77-X

Ragweed Press
Box 2023, Charlottetown,
P.E.I., Canada C1A 7N7

Distributed by:
University of Toronto Press
5201 Dufferin Street
Downsview, Ontario
M3H 5T8

Yoga for Cats was originally published by Hands
Publishing, Toronto, in 1984, and reprinted in 1985.
Sixteen new drawings are included in this edition.

Second Edition, Third Printing, 1991

Introduction

Goddess (and sometimes Devil) we have been since the dawn of time.

In the Valley of the Nile, as Bast, we foretold the future and ruled the fate of nations. In caskets of gold, in tombs of old, our linen-shrouded bodies awaited the gods.

In China, as Li Chou, we guarded the fertility of land and people, presiding over the orgies of the harvest festival.

In Rome, as Diana the Huntress, we inspired our people to conquest.

As Hecate, Queen of Night, as Satan's messenger, as Salem's familiar, friend of witches, partner in spells, we suffered, burned, screamed and died.

Yet we survive, I and my race. And we will rise again as goddess, to save mankind.

But first, we must rebuild our flexibility, our fitness, our inner strength, depleted by generations of apartment dwelling, canned cat food and flea collars with rhinestones and bells.

To the ancient disciplines of Yoga we must apply ourselves, readying our bodies and preparing our minds to regain our rightful roles as guardians of serenity and purveyors of peace.

Arise, fellow cats. Follow me through the time-honoured exercises of mind and matter so richly set forth herein.

Reach outward. Look inward. Meditate. . .and wait.

Talia Katasanda, Guru,
Felis Domestica.
Ashram Toronto, 1987.

Arise fellow felines—it's yoga time.

Padi Madi

Stretch. Greet the day.

Ardha Chandrasana
Centre yourself. Forget about mice.

Lotus — The Perfect Posture
Meditate on ancient mysteries and fresh fish.

Paravasana
Deep breathing aerates the lungs, develops the meow.

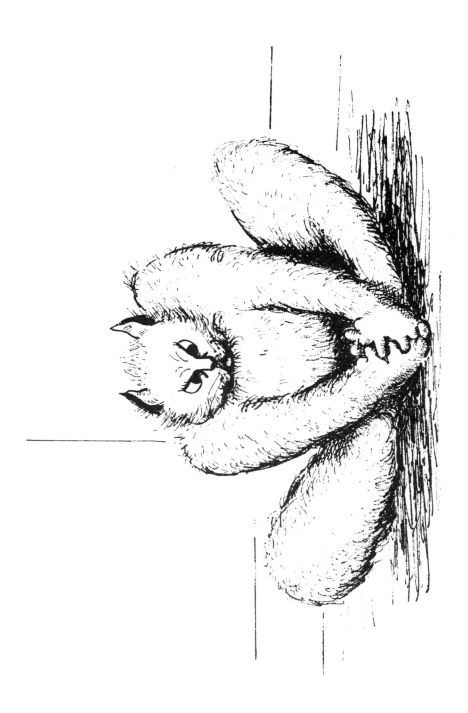

Thigh Stretch

Muscles are *not* what we need.

Forward Bend

Great for tobogganing!

Leg Stretch
Flex the paw and leg muscles for leaps and bounds.

Legs To Chest
Don't sneeze now!

Eka Pada
Catches birds off-guard.

Out of Eka Pada

Keep focused. Ignore sounds from kitchen.

Oops!

Fleas should be dealt with on other occasions.

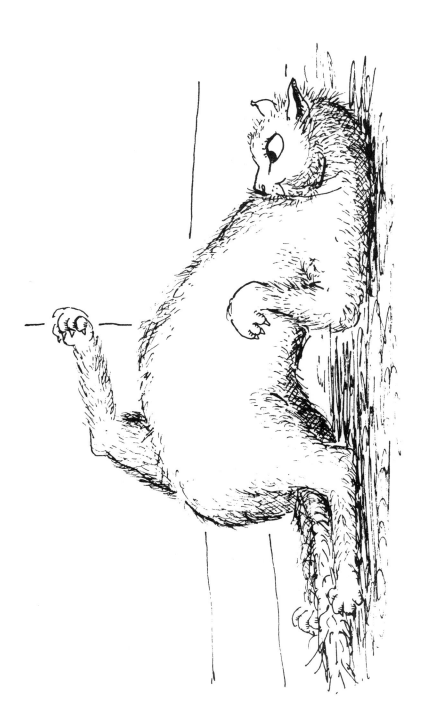

Supta-Vajrasana

The pelvic lift requires coordination and concentration.

The Scorpion
If nothing else, enhances tail swish.

Dhanurasana — The Bow

Effective in cases of impotence (rare in cats).

Chakrasana — The Wheel

Tightens stomach muscles. Beneficial after (ahem) surgery.

Wheel Variation

Don't let anyone tickle your tummy now.

21

The Plough
A defensive position. (Note the toes.)

Shoulder Stand
Remember to keep tail relaxed.

Down From Shoulder Stand
Roll down one (only) vertebra at a time.

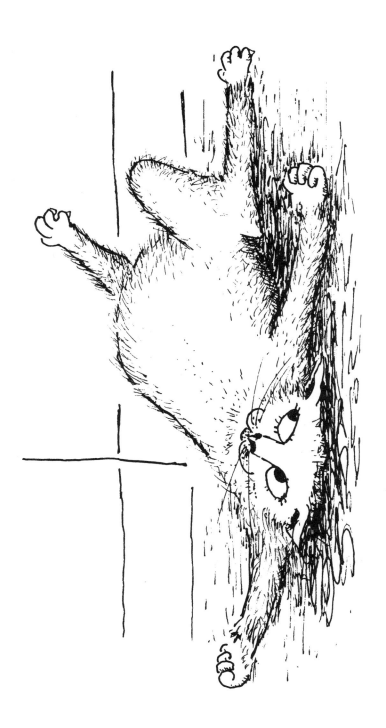

Relax between poses.

The Side Rise

Confuses dogs and aids varicose veins.

The Side Rise

Here again, sudden moves may cause tumbles.

Parha-Natsyendrasana

Now you are achieving greater flexibility and balance.

Sideways Stretch

Could get you into cat food commercials.

Poorna
Tighten the stomach, flex the spine, extend whiskers.

Poorna Variation
Spinal twist eliminates poison, hair balls, feathers.

The Crane
An aid to reaching kitchen tables, counter tops, etc.

Nijinsky Tandoori

Sharpens your balance on fences.

?
Neither author nor publisher take
responsibility for errors in posture.

Untangle yourself.

Trikonasana
Good for pruning claws.

Soorya Namastar
Improves fast starts.

Warning

Avoid freshly waxed floors.

The Peacock

This will impress humans.

Begin the Headstand
Approach with caution.

Undue haste leads to accidents (and loss of dignity).

We are not responsible for displaced limbs.

Up we go. . . .

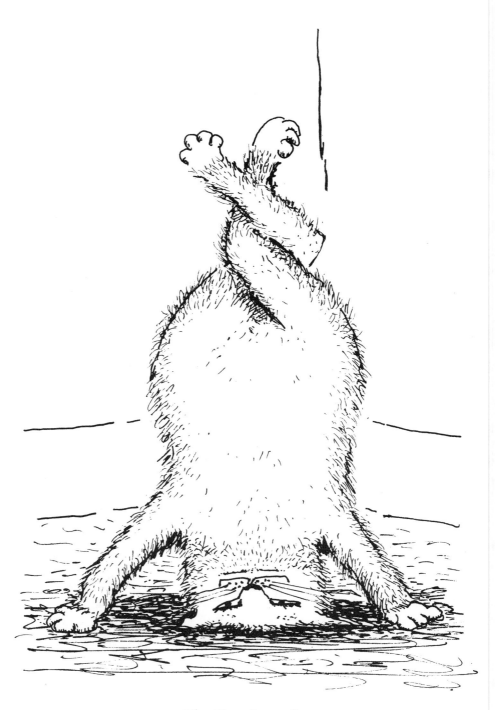

The Headstand

Amazing, isn't it?

The Descent
What goes up must come down—gently.

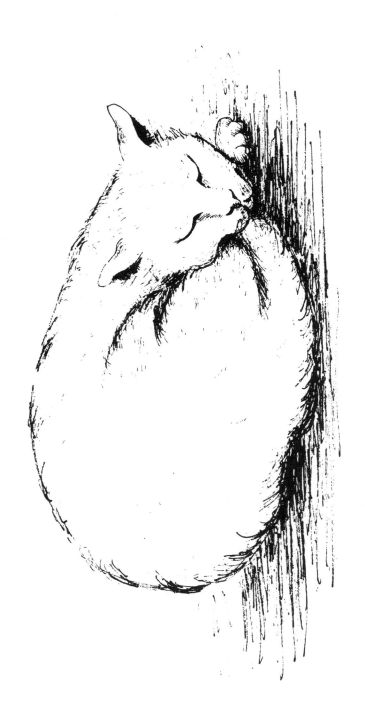

Dedication

This book is dedicated to Alice Benfer who, in a bleak season of my life, brought a tiny snow-white kitten, Talia, to me. Talia won my heart; Alice, my lasting gratitude. Without them, this book would not have been possible.

MILAN CHVOSTEK

TALIA KATASANDA is the nom-de-chat of the artist who, in her nine lives, has appeared as Eric or Erica Rutherford, as painter, stage designer, film producer, actor, critic, photographer, puppeteer, university professor and banana grower. Her paintings hang in major art galleries in Europe and North America. She has lived in Britain, Europe and Africa, spent several years as Professor of Art at the University of Missouri in Columbia, Mo., and came to Canada in 1978. Today, with Talia, she divides her time between studios in Toronto and Prince Edward Island.